INSTANT ACTIVITIES
for
CREATIVE WRITING
That Kids Really Love!

SCHOLASTIC
PROFESSIONAL BOOKS

NEW YORK ◆ TORONTO ◆ LONDON ◆ AUCKLAND ◆ SYDNEY

Edited by Linda Beech. Written by Merrily P. Hansen,
Marty Lee, Tara McCarthy, and Marcia Miller

Cover design by Vincent Ceci and Jaime Lucero

Cover Illustration/photograph by Abby Carter

Interior design by Ellen Matlach Hassell
for Boultinghouse & Boultinghouse, Inc.

Interior illustrations by Teresa Anderko, Rick Brown,
Drew Hires, Holly Kowitt, and Manuel Rivera.

ISBN 0-590-36509-6

Printed in the U.S.A.

12 11 10 9 8 7 6 5 4 3 2 1   7 8 9 / 00 / 01 / 02

CONTENTS

(continued on the next page)

INTRODUCTION

Instant Activities for Creative Writing is an idea book full of exciting ways to get the story*tellers* in your class "talking on paper." You and your students will discover that the projects, activities, and lessons are easy to use and fun to do.

A glance at the table of contents outlines our own story: upbeat materials with up-to-date strategies based on the writing process. You'll find ideas and materials for setting up your classroom to create a rich writers' environment and to get students started thinking like authors. Students will learn how to come up with ideas for their stories and how to choose and use language creatively. Most important, they'll learn how to put their good ideas and creative words to work in a story. They'll learn techniques for structuring a story, developing interesting characters, and creating exciting settings and moods for their stories. Mini-lessons focus on specific skills and can be integrated into your curriculum any time your students are ready.

Good literature supports all the ideas included here. We've used the words of famous authors to model great story openings and endings and what's in between. We've included independent study activities and activities students can do with partners or in cooperative learning groups.

Two start-to-finish, step-by-step creative story-writing projects using the writing process can serve as models for other similar lessons as your young authors become more and more proficient.

Before you begin, be sure sure to display and discuss the poster *Writers Talk About Writing* included with this book. Then let the stories unfold!

SMART STARTS...

...and techniques to use throughout the year

WRITERS' WORKPLACE

Although some students write best when they sit at their own familiar desk or worktable, it can be very inspiring for students to have a place dedicated exclusively to writing. If your classroom space allows, set up a writing center. Here are some ideas to consider.

Independent Activities and Reproducibles

Copy and place the independent student activity reproducibles (pages 58–60) and skills-practice reproducibles (pages 32–39) in the writing center. You may want to laminate the activity reproducibles. Tell students that each of the independent activities addresses a different part of the writing process, and the reproducibles offer independent writing activities. Post a list of the topics so students can see what is available to them. You may choose to assign students to work with one or more of the activity reproducibles in a particular order, or you may leave it to them to consult those they need. You can also present the information from an activity reproducible to the whole class or to a learning group. Use the skills-practice reproducibles in class or for homework. Include appropriate reproducibles as you introduce various lessons.

Eyes on Supplies

Set up an area in the classroom where students have access to paper (lined and unlined), pencils, pens, erasers, correction fluid, file folders, paper clips, pencil sharpeners, a wastebasket, and other writing supplies. You might also include materials for making books. (See page 67.) Stock a nearby bookcase with reference books, such as a dictionary, thesaurus, almanac, and if possible, a set of encyclopedias. Have an assortment of poetry books, folktales, or picture collections students can consult for ideas and inspiration.

Display the poster, *Writers Talk About Writing* (inside back cover). Place students' writing folders, journals, or portfolios in your writing center.

As You Like It

Some teachers have found it effective to make the following aids available in a writers' center:

◆ lists of commonly misspelled words

◆ lists of synonyms for overused words

◆ new word of the day (or week)

◆ books of baby names (a useful resource for naming characters in stories)

◆ *The Guinness Book of Records* (as a source for amazing facts to inspire writers).

Be sure to ask students what materials they would like to include in the center.

Mechanics

In addition to a computer that you may have in your classroom, many students enjoy writing on typewriters. Ask if any families have unused typewriters they are willing to provide on long-term loan while their child is in your class. Be sure to provide typing paper and correcting tape.

WRITERS' WORDS

Writing is all about communication, and in order to communicate clearly, it's important that everyone speak and understand the same language.

The glossary on this page provides definitions of some of the key terms used by writers in discussing their work. You may wish to reproduce these terms and their definitions on a chart for handy reference in class. To give your students hands-on practice in applying these terms and understanding their meanings, try the activities described.

character—person (or sometimes animal) in a story or poem

conclusion—the end of a story in which all the story problems are solved

dialogue—the talking that goes on between characters in a story

fiction—writing not necessarily based on fact

mood—the feeling a reader gets from a piece of writing, for example: happy, sad, scary, peaceful

moral—the lesson taught by the story

narrator—the person or character telling the story

plot—the series of events that make up the action of the story

point of view—angle from which the story is told. A first-person point of view means one of the characters is telling the story. A third-person point of view means that someone outside the story is telling it.

problem—the problems or difficulties that the story characters must solve

setting—the time and place of the story

theme—the message about life that the story is trying to get across

tone—the author's feeling toward the characters and the story. The tone may be serious or funny, or may poke fun at something.

Writers' Terms

Divide the class into twelve writing teams and assign each team one of the terms. Challenge them to do an in-depth exploration of their term and create a poster with excerpts or examples that illustrate the term drawn from stories they've read. Suggest that students sign their names on the poster so they can serve as on-the-spot classroom consultants to help with the interpretation of their term.

Scavenger Hunt

Once teams have reviewed their posters with the class, try a scavenger hunt in which each team is presented with a list of literary elements to locate. An alternative is to share a sample list like the one below. Each team can then produce a similar list to be exchanged with another team in the class.

Writer's Scavenger Hunt

1. Find a story written from a first-person point of view. Describe this storyteller.

2. Find a story in which an animal is an important character. Describe the animal. What role does it play in the story?

3. Find a story where the writer's tone is serious. Is there a moral to the story? What is it?

4. Find a story set in the future. Describe the setting. How does it differ from today?

5. Find a story with a scary mood. How does the writer create this mood?

6. Find examples of humorous dialogue. What makes them funny?

CREATIVE WRITING IS...?

On sticky-pad notes have each student write a sentence that begins "Creative Writing is...." Stick the notes on a poster pad and leave it on display. Encourage students to rewrite or revise their sentences as they gain experience in creative writing.

Who Are Creative Writers?

Brainstorm with the class a list of favorite writers or authors who write fiction. As you list writers' names, have students identify some of their books. Ask them what the writers might have in common. Students may say that creative writers like words, like to tell stories, like to read, or have good imaginations.

Ask students to find out about and report on their favorite authors. They might use references that give biographical sketches on children's authors and illustrators that are listed in the Bibliography on page 72.

Be sure that students understand that they, too, can be creative writers. Before going any farther, you may want to pass out the writing inventory on the next page. This will not only help students focus on their own writing but will give you some insights into students' attitudes as well.

What It Is, What It Isn't

To help students understand what is unique about creative writing, work with the class to create a chart that compares creative writing to other kinds of writing. You might ask questions such as:

◆ Is creative writing always factual? What kinds of writing are?

◆ Is fiction ever based on facts? How?

◆ What is the purpose of creative writing? Of other types of writing?

◆ Who reads creative writing? Who reads other kinds of writing?

◆ What forms does creative writing take? What forms are used in other kinds of writing?

A Writing Environment

The craft of writing takes practice and some basic tools. Have students list their ideal writing tools and writing environments. For instance, some students like to use a sharp pencil, and others prefer felt-tipped pens. Some students like to write to background music, while others prefer quiet. If possible, obtain an assortment of the supplies students like to use and encourage them to bring their own favorites. Vary the classroom writing environment from time to time to suit different writers' styles.

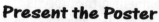

Present the Poster

Display the poster that comes with this book and ask volunteers to read aloud what each writer says. Invite students to comment on these ideas and to add their own. You might post students' writing ideas next to the poster. Because reading is an important link to writing, you might want to have the books mentioned on the poster available in your classroom.

Name_____

WRITING INVENTORY

**Writing means different things to different people.
What does it mean to you? Read the questions.
Check the answers that apply, or write your own answers.**

1. What kind of writer do you think you are?

☐ creative ☐ fair ☐ good ☐ careless

☐ reluctant ☐ thoughtful ☐ excellent ☐ other (explain)

_____

2. When you have a writing assignment, how do you feel?

☐ creative ☐ challenged ☐ happy ☐ worried

☐ other (explain) _____

3. What topics do you like most to write about? Why?

_____

_____

_____

4. What kinds of writing do you do at home?

_____

_____

5. Who are your favorite writers? Why?

_____

_____

_____

6. How do you think you could become a better writer?

_____

_____

More To Try! ➤ **Why is writing an important skill?** _____

_____

START-UP IDEAS AND TIPS

It's in Your Head

A tip professional writers frequently give to students is to write about what they know. Have students list topics of interest to them. You might have students complete a chart like this:

I know a lot about—	I've had experience at—	I'm curious about—

Have students keep their interest inventories with their ongoing writing. They can add to it at any time or consult it for writing ideas.

Springboards

Writing teachers have different views toward providing story starters to students. A concern is that if students are given topics, they will not develop an ability to generate ideas on their own. Here are three effective ways to offer hints for story ideas that are open-ended and student centered.

1. Magazines and Catalogs Sometimes a visual cue can spark a student's imagination. Invite students to browse through magazines or catalogs when they are stuck for an idea.

2. File Folder Visuals When you come across an interesting photograph or illustration, clip it and paste it inside a file folder. Also list some related words or phrases that can stimulate an idea. Store folders in the writing center.

3. Old Postcards Encourage students to contribute old picture postcards to an idea box. Writers can pick a card and base a story on the picture, or weave a tale around the message written on the card.

A New Slant

Encourage students to explore an idea from an unusual perspective. For instance, instead of writing about a vacation from the point of view of a tourist, why not write it from the point of view of the camera that gets lugged from place to place and pointed at different sights?

> **TEACHER TIP**
> Picture books are not only fun to look at, they often offer models of good writing. Students enjoy rereading favorite stories and discovering lyrical language, flights of fantasy, or meaningful situations.

Read!

People who enjoy writing usually also enjoy reading. The more information writers have, the more they can draw upon for their own work. Consider setting aside time at the start of each creative writing session for students to engage in uninterrupted silent reading. There's no telling what inspirations can result from a five- or ten-minute side trip to the world of literature.

Schedule Switching

Some students are more alert in the mornings. Others seem not to come alive until after lunch. Try to vary the times for creative writing to accommodate the variations in your students.

Have some quick-writing sessions—3- to 5-minute bursts of writing to keep students focused as active writers. Naturally, such a short time is not enough to complete a piece or work through a troublesome section of an assignment, but it provides many opportunities to write without the expectations of the full writing process.

PARAGRAPH-WRITING GAME

TEAM STORIES

Here's a story-writing game that students can play in groups. While they're having fun, students will also be getting practice in writing coherent paragraphs. Have each group sit in a circle. Then use these directions to explain how to play. Each student will need a piece of lined paper and a pencil.

1. Think of a first line of a story. Write it on a sheet of lined paper. Try to make your sentence catchy and descriptive. Here's an example: A ship of aliens landed in my backyard last night at midnight.

2. Pass your paper, with the opening sentence on it, to the person on your right. At the same time, you will get a piece of paper from your left with someone else's opening line on it.

3. Read the sentence on the paper you receive. Without discussing, it add a sentence to continue the story. Then pass this paper to your right and get a paper from your left.

4. Continue writing and passing until everyone in the group has contributed a sentence to every story. Stop when you get the paper with your opening sentence on it.

Before students begin, ask them to keep in mind the following:

◆ Add only one sentence at a time.

◆ As a partial story reaches you, be sure to read all of it. Think about its subject, setting, and mood.

◆ The sentence you write must continue the story, but can go off in any direction you wish. Be creative!

◆ Begin a new paragraph if you think one is needed.

◆ If your sentence will be the last one written, try to wrap up the story.

◆ Work independently and as quietly as possible because lots of thinking and writing will be going on all around you.

When the papers have made a full circle, have the members of each group read their completed story aloud. Suggest that the groups add titles to their stories.

Variations

1. Have students start another story. This time, tell them to send the stories around the group twice. **2.** Give students a theme for their stories. Compare how the theme is developed from group to group.

LETTER TO PARENTS

Students love to share their finished work with family members, but you can involve families earlier in the process, too.

◆ Reproduce and send home the letter on this page to inform parents of what students are working on and how they can help.

◆ Enlist parents or other caregivers to come into the classroom to work as computer aides. If students decide to publish their work in a literary magazine format (see page 18), parents might also help with this project.

◆ Take a survey to see if any parents use creative writing in their work. Invite these writers or editors in to speak to the class.

◆ Send home the reproducible on the next page so that family members and friends can read and comment on students' work.

Dear Parent or Caregiver,

We are doing a lot of creative writing in class right now and hope that you will help us. Here are three ways you can help:

1. Read with your child. Studies have shown a direct link between reading aloud to children of all ages and their learning to write. Older children who are already readers can still gain in many ways from this shared reading experience. In addition, whenever possible, let your child see YOU reading. By offering this kind of model, you are giving the message that literacy is important and fun.

2. Support your child's efforts. Young writers, in fact all writers, need lots of encouragement. Praise for and discussion of his or her writing lets your child know just how much you appreciate the effort.

3. Share your family's stories. Experience is a rich source for all writers, and family stories are an important part of a child's life. Sharing these stories will offer your child wonderful ideas to write about and to have for a lifetime.

Thank you so much for your support. Your attention and interest will help your child achieve the very best!

Sincerely,

Name_____

PLEASE COMMENT

Choose something that you have written. Make a clean copy. Then share your work with members of your family, friends, neighbors, or classmates. Ask each reader to write a thoughtful comment. Use the form on this page. Save your comment sheet in your journal or writer's notebook.

MY STORY TITLE: _____

Comments	Signatures
Your story has a powerful beginning. I really wanted to read more.	Dad
I learned a lot about fishing from this story.	Mr. Burns

STORY-SHARING BULLETIN BOARD

For many writers one of the most important aspects of writing is the pride of ownership that comes with sharing their work. Here's a simple bulletin board idea that will enable students to take turns displaying their stories.

Materials:

craft paper ◆ colored markers ◆ tacks ◆ paper clips ◆ instant camera (optional)

Steps:

1. Cover a bulletin board with bright craft paper. At the top write the title STORY SURPRISES in magic marker.

2. Duplicate and enlarge the patterns on the next page. Add a gift box for each student to the bulletin board.

3. Students can fold their stories accordion style. On the top fold they write the story title and their name.

4. Show students how to fasten their folded stories together with a paper clip.

5. Tack the bottom fold of the stories inside the box outlines as shown. To read a story, simply remove the paper clip and unfold the page.

6. For fun, take a picture of each class author with an instant camera. Place the developed photos next to the students' stories with brief captions.

Story Surprises

Henry's Bike Swap

CLASS CLOWN

LITERARY MAGAZINE

As a culminating project, you might have students publish a literary magazine to showcase their creative writing efforts. If you have access to a desktop publishing program, this is an authentic application of the technology skills students are learning. If you're not yet "booted up," your class can still produce a magazine that they'll be proud to share and save for many years to come.

Here are some suggestions for launching the project.

◆ To begin, you might display samples of literary magazines produced by past classes and encourage students to browse through them. Then give students an easy-to-understand overview of the publishing process by sharing Aliki's *How a Book Is Made* (Bantam, 1986).

◆ Brainstorm the jobs needed to publish a literary magazine. Record the tasks that students mention on a chart posted in the classroom. While everyone is a contributing author, students can also work as illustrators, designers and layout specialists, keyboarders or typists, proofreaders, paste-up specialists, duplicators and collators, and ad copywriters.

◆ After exploring the responsibilities associated with each job, invite students to volunteer for work assignments. (You might rotate these assignments to ensure that everyone has an opportunity to work on more than one aspect of the project.) As a first task, have each group work together to write a detailed job description outlining their roles and responsibilities.

◆ Ask students to look over recent writing assignments in their portfolios. Then invite each student to select one piece to contribute to the literary magazine. Students should choose the assignment they like best, regardless of length or genre.

◆ Now the work of producing and assembling the magazine begins. To guide the process, consider developing a flowchart and schedule with your class. You may even wish to ask several students to take on the job of "trafficking" the manuscript and art as they travel from one step to the next in the production process. This is also a great time to take advantage of parent volunteers who are willing to work with small groups on different aspects of magazine.

◆ When the bound literary magazines have finally rolled off the presses, hold a gala publication party to introduce your magazine to parents and the school community! Invite your authors to read aloud their work.

SKILLS-PRACTICE MINI-LESSONS...

...to use as your creative writers need them

HE SAID, SHE SAID

Students enjoy including dialogue when they write, but they often have trouble writing it clearly. These techniques use literature to highlight dialogue.

Present this excerpt on the chalkboard or on an overhead transparency.

> I t was the beginning of autumn when Sadako rushed home with the good news. She kicked off her shoes and threw open the door with a bang. "I'm home!" she called.
>
> Her mother was fixing supper in the kitchen.
>
> "The most wonderful thing has happened!" Sadako said breathlessly. "Guess what!"
>
> "Many wonderful things happen to you, Sadako chan. I can't even guess."
>
> "The big race on Field Day!" Sadako said. "I've been chosen from the bamboo class to be on the relay team." She danced around the room, gaily swinging her school bag. "Just think. If we win, I'll be sure to get on the team in junior high school next year." That was what Sadako wanted more than anything else.

Excerpt from *Sadako and the Thousand Paper Cranes* by Eleanor Coerr. Text copyright © 1977 by Eleanor Coerr. Used by permission of G.P. Putnam's Sons.

Discuss with students how they know who is speaking. They may cite the quotation marks that begin and end the exact words a person says as well as phrases that tell who is speaking, such as *she called* or *Sadako said*.

Students may notice that not every quotation identifies the speaker. Introduce the rule of starting a new paragraph when another person speaks. This rule gives readers three clues to know who says "Many wonderful things happen to you...."

◆ Only Sadako and her mother are in this scene.

◆ Sadako has just spoken.

◆ A new paragraph has begun.

Therefore, Sadako's mother must be speaking.

Listen Here!

Have one volunteer read the excerpt aloud in an expressive way. Then ask two volunteers to read only the dialogue, as if this were a scene from a play. Use this technique with other literature excerpts, including those that feature more than two speakers.

Literature Search

Ask students to find excerpts with dialogue from other books. Suggest that students use three different sources, or find three excerpts from the same source. Invite students to take turns presenting their dialogue.

Descriptor Detectives

Suggest that students find different ways that authors describe who is speaking, or how they speak. Collect examples on a list to post in the creative writing center. Students can refer to the list to spark up their own dialogue writing with phrases such as

◆ gasped Marcia   ◆ Malik retorted

◆ she snapped   ◆ he hesitated

Name_____

CAN WE HAVE A DIALOGUE?

In real life, people talk a lot. So people talk in stories too. This is called dialogue. Have you ever noticed that most of the words in cartoons are dialogue?

Here's a chance to practice your dialogue skills.
Pretend you are a cartoonist and write dialogue for these scenes.

1. Read what this girl says to her friend. Write what the friend might say in response.

_____

_____

_____

2. What did the boy hear before he answered? Write what the girl might have told him.

_____

_____

_____

3. Two friends are discussing a new movie. What might they be saying? Write the dialogue.

Girl: _____

_____

Boy: _____

_____

Add another cartoon "cell" (box) to each scene above. Write more dialogue for the characters to say.

GREAT OPENINGS

The beginning of a story is an invitation. It is the way a writer asks readers to "come in and enjoy themselves." One way to write good beginnings is to study what others have done. Here are some examples of different kinds of openings that you can share with the class.

A Little Mystery

Keith, the boy in the rumpled shorts and shirt, did not know he was being watched as he entered room 215 of the Mountain View Inn.

from *The Mouse and the Motorcycle* by Beverly Cleary

A Promising Conversation

Hey, Tom! Where were you last night?" "Yeah, you missed it.

from *How to Eat Fried Worms* by Thomas Rockwell

Something Curious

Melinda Pratt rides city bus number twelve to her cello lesson, wearing her mother's jean jacket and only one sock.

from *The Facts and Fictions of Minna Pratt* by Patricia MacLachlan

Something Silly

Once there was a boy called Jacob Two-Two.

from *Jacob Two-Two Meets the Hooded Fang* by Mordecai Richler

A Memorable Memory

I remember the day the Aleut ship came to our island.

from *Island of the Blue Dolphins* by Scott O'Dell

From Reading to Writing

Follow up by using these activities with the class.

1. Ask students to find one or two other story openings for each category.

2. Have students make a list of questions that each of the openings on this card suggests to them. For example, after reading the quote from The Mouse and the Motorcycle, they might write: Who is watching Keith? Why is Keith being watched?

3. Suggest that students visit your school or public library and find five more story openings that appeal to them. Students can copy these into a notebook.

4. Under each story opening, have students write why they liked it.

5. Have students write story beginnings of their own and share them with partners.

GREAT ENDINGS

"All's well that ends well." You can use literature to help students focus on story endings. You might suggest that students think of their stories as gifts and their story endings as ways to wrap up the story-gifts. Present these examples for the class to discuss. Then ask students to find other examples of each kind of ending to share with the class.

1. The Happy-Ending Wrapper

Then at last the Rough-Face girl and the Invisible Being were married. They lived together in great gladness and were never parted.

> Excerpt from *The Rough-Face Girl* by Rafe Martin, illustrated by David Shannon. Text copyright © 1992 by Rafe Martin. Used by permission of G. P. Putnam's Sons.

2. The Sad-But-True Wrapper

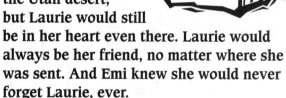

Emi knew Mama was right. They would soon be sent to a camp in the Utah desert, but Laurie would still be in her heart even there. Laurie would always be her friend, no matter where she was sent. And Emi knew she would never forget Laurie, ever.

> Excerpt from *The Bracelet* by Yoshiko Uchida, illustrated by Joanna Yardley. Text copyright © 1976, 1993 by Yoshiko Uchida. Used by permission of Philomel Books.

3. The Summarizing-Everything Wrapper

It is not often that someone comes along who is a true friend and a good writer. Charlotte was both.

> from *Charlotte's Web* by E. B. White

In your discussion ask students to consider: How does each kind of ending make them feel? What was the author's intent? How does the ending wrap up the story?

At the End

Have students go through books they've enjoyed and find endings that they think are especially great. After students share their endings with the class, challenge them to classify the endings on a chart. If necessary, have students identify other types of endings. With the class develop some features of a good story ending. Post these in your writing center along with some books that have such endings.

Ask students to reread endings that they have recently used in their stories. How could they make their endings stronger?

Kinds of Endings			
Happy	Sad-But-True	Summarizing	Satisfying

You'll find a "Story Middles" reproducible on page 63.

MEET THE AUTHOR: PATRICIA REILLY GIFF

For more author inspiration, see the poster, *Writers Talk About Writing.*

Share this information about Patricia Reilly Giff with the class.

Born in Brooklyn, New York, on April 26, 1935, Patricia Reilly Giff knew as a child that she wanted to write, but she suffered feelings of insecurity about whether she was good enough. The fear that people might laugh at her work kept her from sharing it with others. When she reached her 40th birthday, she decided that she would write a story—even if it took the rest of her life. It did not take forever to write this first book, but it did take a long time!

People, Places, Problems

How does Giff begin a book? She follows three simple steps. First she thinks of a person. She never picks someone who is perfect—that would be too boring. Instead she thinks about students she had in school as a teacher; she also thinks about her own three children and their friends. She tries to picture someone who has some interesting failings—someone who is funny, lively, and maybe a little mischievous—someone who's "zippy!"

Once she has a picture of the character in her mind, Giff works on dropping that person into a place that she's very familiar with. For someone with her background, it's often a school or a family setting. Last, but not least, she gives the character a problem that has to be solved.

When asked what she thinks her greatest writing strength is, Giff identifies her ability to write natural-sounding dialogue. Not only is she a great listener to what is said, but she also has an uncanny ability to remember exact conversations that occurred 25 years ago!

Learning from a Writer

Once you've shared this information about Patricia Reilly Giff, suggest that students try these activities to see if her writing strategies work for them.

◆ To write more natural sounding dialogue, suggest that students listen to the way that people really talk. Students can use a tape recorder to help them remember what they hear. Then have them write a conversation.

◆ Giff believes that practice makes perfect. Encourage your students to practice their writing for a short period (for example, ten minutes) every day. Like any good habit, it's easier to do if it becomes part of a routine.

◆ Review Giff's three simple steps for starting a book. Your students might even want to try her technique of lying in the middle of the living room rug as she visualizes her character, setting, and story problem!

◆ Encourage students to share their writing freely with all who want to read it. Remind them that Giff went for years without writing because she was too afraid to share her work with others.

Be sure to show students the revised draft from Patricia Reilly Giff's book, *The Candy Corn Contest,* on the next page.

Making It Better

Students may not realize that every writer, no matter how experienced, almost always reworks what's been written. By sharing the draft and final edited version of a manuscript by Patricia Reilly Giff, students will see how a draft can change before it's finally published. This example is from the first chapter of *The Candy Corn Contest*. Here are a few ways you can use this authentic material.

◆ Begin by showing students just the edited draft. Can they interpret the editing marks? What do they mean? What will the final copy look like based on the changes that are marked? Using the explanation of editing marks on page 66, challenge students to create the final version. Then have them check their final copy against the published book copy.

◆ Suggest that pairs of students take the parts of Giff and her editor and role-play an editing conference. Using the edited draft copy, have them confer about the proposed changes. Why is each change being made? How does it help to improve the copy? Is there another alternative that might work?

◆ Have students recall Giff's three-step process for starting a story, described on page 24. *(Visualize the character, setting, and story problem.)* From these opening lines in the first chapter of this book, what can they tell about the character and the setting? Do they have any hints about what the story problem might be from the title of the story?

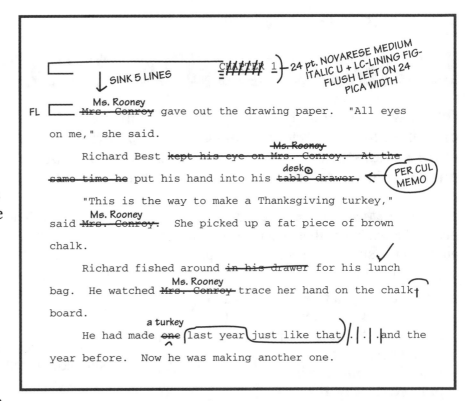

Ms. Giff started with the draft above, which she then edited to create the final book copy below.

Chapter 1

Ms. Rooney gave out the drawing paper. "All eyes on me," she said.

Richard Best put his hand into his desk.

"This is the way to make a Thanksgiving turkey," said Ms. Rooney. She picked up a fat piece of brown chalk.

Richard fished around for his lunch bag. He watched Ms. Rooney trace her hand on the chalkboard.

He had made a turkey just like that last year . . . and the year before. Now he was making another one.

USING SPECIFIC WORDS

One way to show details is by using specific words. To stress the utility and fun of being specific, try the following group activities, which are given in approximate easier-to-more-difficult sequence. After each activity, invite students to put their insights to work in an independent or shared writing assignment.

1. The I-Dunno Secret Object

Before the activity, without students' knowledge, put an object such as Frisbee in a large paper bag. Tell students:

> I have a thing in this bag. It has a shape. It has a color. It has a size. It's made of a material. People use it in a certain way. It's like something else. What is it?

Ask students why it's difficult to guess the object from this description. Then present a revised description, for example:

> I have a <u>toy</u> in this bag. It's <u>round</u>. It's <u>white and blue</u>. It's about <u>the size of a plate</u>. It's made of <u>plastic and rubber</u>. People <u>throw it back and forth</u>. It's like <u>a flying saucer</u>.

Most students should be able to identify the object from your second description. Ask them to identify the specific words and phrases that clued them in. Write the clues (underlined in the example) on the chalkboard, using the term *specific* as you do so.

Next, ask students to take turns presenting—in writing or orally—a description of another common object without naming the object. Stress that the purpose of the description is to get the audience to identify the object quickly. Again, have the audience name the specific clues.

2. The Many-Ways Chart

Reproduce the following chart, headings, and first column entries on the chalkboard for the class, and on paper for students or partners to use afterwards. Examples you might use in your chalkboard warm-up are given. Help students determine how the chart entries move from the general to the very specific.

Very general	More specific	Even more specific	Even more and more specific!
a living thing	a plant	a tomato plant	a tomato vine with big, juicy tomatoes hanging on it
a living thing	a human being	a tiny baby	a tiny baby laughing at a clown

Invite students to use their copies of the chart to tell about other living things. Then have students use their charts to develop descriptive sentences, for example: *Wow, was I happy about my garden! There was my tomato vine with big, juicy tomatoes hanging on it!* Some students will enjoy trying other "general" entries, such as *an insect, furniture, food,* or *a sound.*

3. What Nonsense!
"Burgess" Summaries

In Burgess summaries (named for American humorist Frank Gelett Burgess, who loved nonsense and wrote "I never saw a purple cow…"), nonsense words are substituted for actual ones. Readers or listeners must think of sensible, precise, real words to replace the silly words and fit in the context of the sentences. You can introduce this activity to the class by copying the following paragraph (with the nonsense words underlined). Explain that the paragraph is based on *Sarah, Plain and Tall.* Challenge students to think of commonsense substitutes. Possible responses are shown in parentheses. Read the paragraph through at least once before having students try to figure out the nonsense words.

> A <u>fleeg</u> *(woman)* named Sarah goes to live on a <u>glurkle</u> *(farm)*. There she meets two <u>grumsies</u> *(children)* who like her right away. The <u>grumsies</u> *(children; boy and girl)* are afraid that Sarah may <u>crackie</u> *(leave)* them. So they do everything they can to make Sarah <u>crodle</u> *(like)* the <u>glurkle</u> *(farm)*. But when Sarah gets a <u>pluble</u> *(railroad, train)* ticket, they fear she has gone back to <u>schum</u> *(Maine, her old home)*.

How do the words students use to replace the nonsense ones make clear the meaning of the paragraph?

Students—independently, with partners, or in small groups—can use the activity on page 33 to practice substituting real words for nonsense ones.

4. Synonym Hound Hunt

While most students can think of antonyms for a word, they may still have difficulty coming up with synonyms for overused words. Have students work with partners to find synonyms for a list of "tired" words such as the ones below. Beforehand, model how to use resources such as a thesaurus and dictionary.

kind	nice	sweet	interesting	exciting
like	old	fine	wonderful	bad
funny	happy	great	okay	said

SAMES AND OPPOSITES

Understanding synonyms, antonyms, and analogies will help students enliven their writing by using a variety of words. They'll also be better prepared to tackle similar tasks on standardized tests. Follow these steps to explain synonyms and antonyms and how to complete analogies.

1. Begin by asking students to tell how these groups are alike.

tremendous	violet	amble
huge	lavender	stroll
big	plum	march
great	lilac	saunter
(large in size)	*(shades of purple)*	*(ways to walk)*

pleased	exclaim
joyful	shout
cheerful	yell
delighted	holler
(happy)	*(making a loud noise)*

Encourage students to act out or find an example of each word in a group. Once students have discovered the commonality of each group, point out that words with the same or similar meaning are called synonyms. Explain that synonyms often appear in tests called analogies.

2. Use an example with the same words to show what an analogy is.

   Tremendous is to *huge* as *pleased* is to *joyful.*

Ask students to identify two pairs of words *(tremendous/huge, pleased/joyful)* and to tell what their relationship is.

When students are ready, give them an example like this:

   Amble is to *stroll* as *shout* is to _____.

Again, have students identify the relationship of the first pair of words. Then ask them what kind of word is needed to complete the second pair of words with the same relationship. *(synonym)* Be sure students understand that they can complete this statement with *exclaim, yell,* or *holler* because they are all synonyms of *shout.*

3. Next, present some synonym analogies in test format.

   Lilac is to plum as great is to _____.
   a. little   b. large   c. purple

Model the process: "Let's see, the first word pair is lilac and plum. They are both colors for purple so they are synonyms. Now I know that the missing word in the second pair must be a synonym too." Have students look closely at the answer choices. Ask: "Why doesn't *little* complete the analogy? *(It's the opposite, not the same as* great.*)* Why is large a good choice? *(It's a synonym of* great.*)* Why is purple wrong? *(It's a synonym of the first pair of words but not of* great.*)*

4. Introduce antonyms with picture "fractions" such as these:

Then use the words in antonym analogies and follow the same procedure.

5. Explain that many tests are set up so that the test taker has to color in the square or circle of the correct response. Demonstrate these examples:

   Tremendous is to huge as tiny is to _____.
   ⓐ big   ⓑ little   ⓒ funny

   Day is to night as up is to _____.
   ⓐ down   ⓑ high   ⓒ noon

WHO IS SPEAKING?

As you know, voice refers to the point of view from which a story is told. The challenge for many young writers is to keep the voice consistent. Here are some ways you can introduce voice and the value of consistency.

First-Person Voice

The main character speaks as *I*. All the things that happen are told from *I*'s point of view. Make copies of the following example and ask students to find the pronouns (underlined) that make it clear that *I* is the speaker.

It is truly summer and every day <u>we</u> frolic in the sun. Today <u>we</u> launched fleets of purple mussel shells on the still pools that the tides have left among the rocks. These pools remind <u>me</u> of pieces of fallen rainbow because they hold seaweeds colored crimson, green, and violet. Rosy and lilac starfish cling to their sides. <u>We</u> laughed to see two hermit crabs fight over a moon shell. With the crab and limpet, the grasshopper and cricket, <u>we</u> are friends and neighbors.

from *Celia's Island Journal* by Loretta Krupinski. Copyright © 1992 by Loretta Krupinski. By permission of Little, Brown & Co.

Class Activity Provide students with this model to discuss and revise for consistency of first-person voice. Discuss how consistency makes the revision clearer than the model.

It was a glorious day, so I decided to plant a garden. He gathered up some seed packs and a trowel and a hoe. Then I called my friend to come over. We worked for about an hour and then they decided it was time for lemonade.

Group Activity Ask groups of students to find examples of first-person voice in books they've read. Students can take turns reading the selections aloud.

Partner Activity Suggest that partners write a paragraph using the first-person voice. Invite students to read their paragraphs to a larger group. Ask the audience to listen for consistency.

Third-Person Voice

This is the voice or point of view that most students use. In the third-person voice, the story is told by an outside "narrator." Readers see things and events as that person sees them. Here's an example to share with students.

Br'er Rabbit thought and thought about how to escape from Br'er Fox. How could he do it? After all, he knew Br'er Fox was strong and determined. "Ah, ha!" said Br'er Rabbit. "Maybe the ol' briar patch trick will work!"

Partner Activity Encourage students to think about voice or point of view as they revise their own stories. Have they made that voice consistent throughout? Writers may work with partners to check for consistency.

MORE
Story-Writing Skills-Practice
REPRODUCIBLES...

**...to use at just the right moment
and in your writing center**

Name_____

WORDS WANTED GAME

Here's a game you can play with a friend.
All you need is a pencil and paper.

Ask your friend to number the paper from 1 to 25. Then have your friend listen as you read each numbered description under the blanks in the story below.

Your friend's job is to write the kind of word called for in each blank. Then for a good laugh, read the story aloud and have your partner insert the words from the list.

The Best Vacation Ever

Last _____, my family and I took a _____ week vacation to
(1. month)   (2. number)
_____. We had a _____ time! During the first part of our
(3. city)   (4. adjective)
trip, we stayed at my _____'s house. He's a great cook! One day for
(5. male relative)
_____ I ate _____ _____. They tasted
(6. meal)   (7. number)   (8. food: plural)
_____! I was so stuffed that they had to pick me up and put me on a
(9. adjective)
_____. We spent the next few days in _____, where we
(10. piece of furniture)   (11. city)
_____. I couldn't believe my _____ when I saw
(12. verb: past tense)   (13. body part)
_____ who was walking down _____ Street with
(14. friend's name)   (15. name of tree)
_____! The star was wearing _____
(16. movie star's name)   (17. number)
_____. I was so surprised that I couldn't even say "_____!"
(18. jewelry)   (19. greeting)
Instead, I just _____ my _____. All too soon, our
(20. verb: past tense)   (21. body part)
vacation was over and it was time to return to _____. I can hardly wait
(22. hometown)
until next _____ when we plan to go to _____.
(23. season)   (24. resort)
There we're sure to run into kids from _____.
(25. name of school)

More To Try! ▶ Try writing your own fill-in story. One approach is to write a story, then go through it replacing certain words with blanks. Figure out a clue for each blank and write it under the blank.

Name_____

WELL, IMAGINE THAT...!

Some observers from another galaxy are watching a traffic jam on Earth. These observers have their own language, so some words in their report are nothing like yours.

There's a <u>cropiss</u> on <u>thrungo</u> number <u>blipple</u>. The <u>cropiss</u> has been caused by a <u>groll</u> colliding with a <u>slamphor</u>. The motorists are feeling very <u>thrumbie</u>, and they are all <u>dracking</u> their horns. We can see one motorist <u>florping</u> his <u>arko</u> and running <u>goppily</u> away from the scene. Thankfully, the <u>schuz</u> have arrived and are helping to direct <u>puliters</u>. We are <u>jungly</u> that we don't have situations like this on our planet!

Translate the report, using your own Earthling words for the ones that are underlined. Be as precise as you can, because this traffic jam is a humdinger! Everyone on Earth should hear about it.

_____

_____

_____

_____

_____

_____

_____

_____

More To Try! ➤ Add at least three adjectives to your paragraph. Choose words that help make the meaning even clearer.

Name_____

TRACKING THE TREASURE

Look what you've found. It's a treasure map!

Study the map. Then think of some answers to these questions. Jot them down on scrap paper.

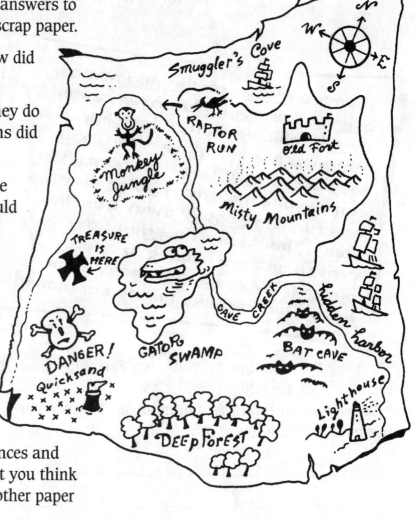

◆ Where did you find the map? How did it get there?

◆ Who made this map? When did they do it? Why did they do it? What plans did they have for using it?

◆ What would you have to do to use this map? What preparations would you make? What problems might you find? What adventure might you have?

◆ What is the treasure? Where did it come from? Why was it hidden?

◆ How would your treasure trip turn out?

Turn your treasure map ideas into a tale. Think of some opening sentences and write them here. Choose the one that you think is best. Then continue the story on other paper

_____

_____

_____

_____

_____

Describe the route you take to follow the map. Use direction words such as *north*, *south*, *east*, and *west*, as well as position words like *behind*, *under*, *beside*, *below*, or *between*. Ask a classmate to follow your directions.

Name_____

WHAT HAPPENED HERE?

Have you ever seen something that you couldn't explain at first? Often, if you think about it and use your imagination, you'll be able to figure it out.

Suppose you are skiing. You see this unusual sight. How did it happen?

One possible solution: The skier was very tall and simply skied right over the tree.

Think of other solutions to this puzzle. Be imaginative! Have some fun with your ideas.

1. _____

2. _____

3. _____

What's the story here? Write your solutions below.

4. _____

_____

_____

5. _____

_____

_____

6. _____

_____

_____

 **More To Try!** Choose the solution you like best. Write a story about it.

Name_____

SET DOWN THE SETTING

An important part of any story is *where* it happens. This is called the *setting*.

Imagine that you take a hot-air balloon ride. During your trip the balloon lands in two different places. What do you see, hear, and even smell in each place? What is it like to be there?

Write a description of each place. Describe it so someone who has never been there can "see" the setting clearly.

1. _____

_____

_____

_____

_____

_____

_____

2. _____

_____

_____

_____

_____

_____

_____

 **More To Try!**

Describe another setting where the hot-air balloon takes you. Ask a classmate to draw a picture of this setting. Is it the same place that you wrote about?

Name_____

GET IN THE MOOD

Imagine that you and your dog are about to enter a dark cave. As you aim your flashlight, a bat flies out. You hear a shriek and a growl, and then you slip and scrape your knee...

How would you describe the **mood** of this scene? Do the words *creepy*, *eerie*, or *terrifying* come to mind? Mood is a way to describe the atmosphere, feelings, or emotions that go with a scene.

Different scenes reflect different moods. Words like *scary, merry, angry, glum, excited,* or *thoughtful* all describe different moods.

Look through magazines to find three photos. Each should show a different mood. Then write a caption for each photo to describe the mood it shows.

Photo 1: _____

_____

_____

Photo 2: _____

_____

_____

Photo 3: _____

_____

_____

Clip the photos to the back of this page.
Challenge a friend to match each photo with its caption.

 **More To Try!** Write a caption for a scene you imagine in your mind. Draw the scene to fit the mood, or find a picture that fits the scene.

Name_____

LITERATURE LINK

YOU ARE THERE

Words can "paint" pictures.
What do you "see" when you read this paragraph?

A fish jumped. Not a large fish, but it made a big splash near the beaver, and as if by a signal there were suddenly little splops all over the side of the lake—along the shore—as fish began jumping. Hundreds of them, jumping and slapping the water. Brian watched them for a time, still in the half-daze, still not thinking well. The scenery was very pretty, he thought, and there were new things to look at, but it was all a green and blue blur and he was used to the gray and black of the city, the sounds of the city. Traffic, people, talking, sounds all the time—the hum and whine of the city.

Excerpt from *Hatchet* by Gary Paulsen. Copyright © 1987 by Gary Paulsen. Reprinted with the permission of Simon & Schuster Books for Young Readers, an imprint of Simon & Schuster Children's Publishing Division.

1. Underline the details that create a "you are there" feeling to the scene.

2. What do you think happened before this scene? Why? _____

_____

3. Brian thinks about the city. Write a paragraph that "paints" a picture of the city.

_____

_____

_____

_____

_____

More To Try!   **Gary Paulsen describes two kinds of sounds in his paragraph.**
Add sounds to your paragraph.

Name_____

COME TO YOUR SENSES

**Step into this picture. Look around you. What do you *see*?
Sniff. What do you *smell*. Listen. What do you *hear*?
Get something to eat. What does it *taste* like?
Pet one of the animals. What do you *feel*?**

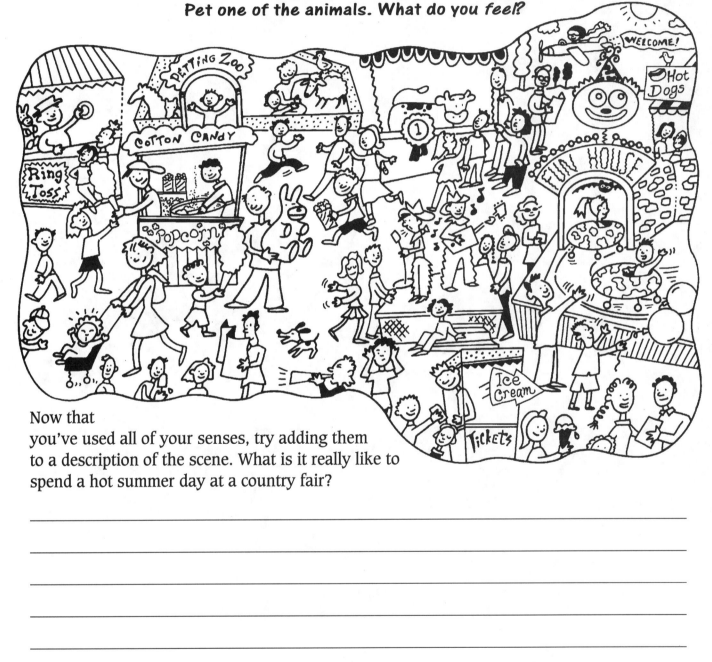

Now that
you've used all of your senses, try adding them
to a description of the scene. What is it really like to
spend a hot summer day at a country fair?

_____

_____

_____

_____

_____

More To Try! **Read your paragraph to someone who has not seen the picture. Can the reader draw the scene based on what you've written? How does the drawing compare with the picture?**

TWO STEP-BY-STEP PROJECTS...

...to get your students thinking and writing with flair

PROJECT 1: CHARACTER STUDY
    Developing a Fictional Character

PROJECT 2: A WHY STORY
    Writing a *Pourquoi* Story

CHARACTER STUDY

For this six-assignment project students will develop a fictional character that they can use in one of their own stories.

Getting Started

Select several literary characters that students already know. For example:

◆ David from *The Wonderful Flight to the Mushroom Planet* by Eleanor Cameron

◆ Mr. Quimby from *Ramona and Her Father* by Beverly Cleary

◆ James from *James and the Giant Peach* by Roald Dahl

◆ Pippi from *Pippi Longstocking* by Astrid Lindgren

Have on hand copies of the books in which the characters appear. You might also consider excerpting vivid descriptions of book characters on poster paper. Or you might use this excerpt:

Character	Book	Appearance	Personality
Laura Ingalls	The Little House Books	- braided brown hair - short - strong body - plain (she says) - tanned skin - twinkling eyes	- stubborn - smart - kind - courageous - hard-working - a bit mischievous
Encyclopedia Brown	The Encyclopedia Brown Books	- short, brown hair - glasses - slight build	- intellectual - hard working - self-employed - law abiding - intuitive

Her hair, the color of a carrot, was braided in two tight braids that stuck out. Her nose was the shape of a very small potato and was dotted all over with freckles. It must be admitted that the mouth under this nose was a very wide one, with strong white teeth. Her dress was rather unusual. Pippi herself had made it. She had meant it to be blue, but there wasn't quite enough blue cloth, so Pippi had sewed little red pieces on it here and there. On her long thin legs she wore a pair of long stockings, one brown and the other black, and she had on a pair of black shoes that were exactly twice as long as her feet. These shoes her father had bought for her in South America so that Pippi would have something to grow into, and she never wanted to wear any others.

Talking About the Task

Use the book characters to introduce the assignment. Begin by asking students to think of how they would describe each character. You might create a chart with students' comments and use it to compare how different authors develop characters. Be sure that students describe both a character's appearance and personality. Follow up by reading aloud character descriptions from the books you have chosen. If you have copied these onto poster paper, display them as models. Encourage students to infer personality traits from the descriptions. If necessary, pose questions to guide students' thinking. As they respond, have students indicate what part of the text gave them that impression. Here are some questions you might ask about Pippi Longstocking:

◆ How do you think Pippi feels about her appearance? Why?

◆ What does the design of Pippi's dress suggest about the way she solves problems?

◆ How do you think Pippi feels about her father? Why?

◆ What does this paragraph tell you about Pippi's father? How might that affect her?

FIRST ASSIGNMENT
Prewriting

Ask students to think of a character they might write about. Suggest that they focus on the character's facial features and personality traits. Then duplicate and enlarge the outline on this page so that each student has a copy (or you might have students make their own). Have students draw in the facial features for their character. Then have them write personality traits within the body outline.

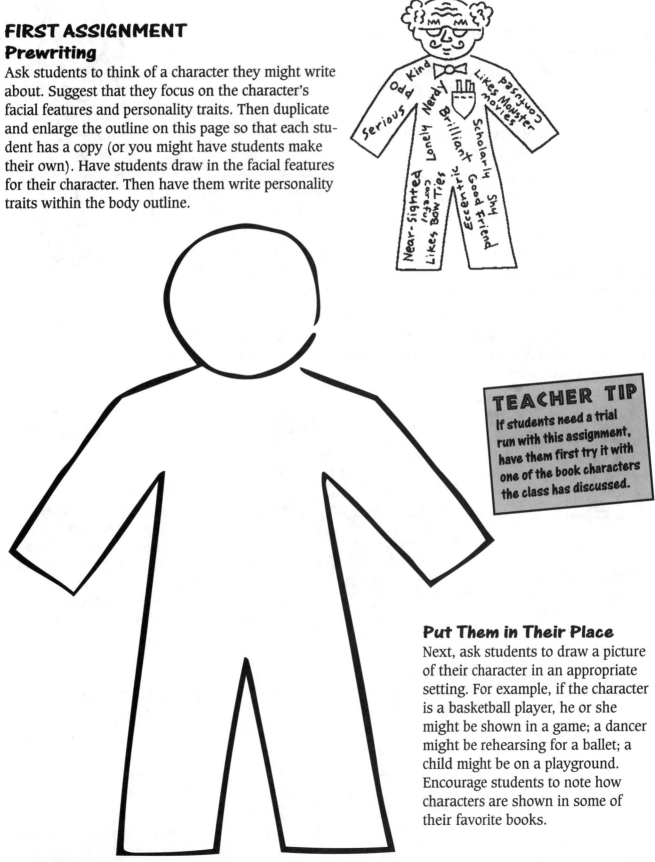

TEACHER TIP
If students need a trial run with this assignment, have them first try it with one of the book characters the class has discussed.

Put Them in Their Place

Next, ask students to draw a picture of their character in an appropriate setting. For example, if the character is a basketball player, he or she might be shown in a game; a dancer might be rehearsing for a ballet; a child might be on a playground. Encourage students to note how characters are shown in some of their favorite books.

SECOND ASSIGNMENT
Prewriting

Have students write or dictate a description of their character, based on the drawings they made. It will probably be a quite literal description of the drawing. For example:

The basketball player is sitting on the bench.
She's watching the game.

Discuss students' drawings with them. Ask questions to help students creatively develop their character. For example, in discussing a picture of a baskeball player, you might ask and comment: What does this person think about basketball? I wonder what she's feeling and thinking as she sits there on the bench. Has she already played in this game, or is she waiting to play?

Ask students to write or dictate a revised description of their characters, based on the insights that the discussion has evoked. In most cases, this revised description will plumb deeper aspects of the character—aspects that go beyond the readily observable. For example:

The player really wants to play in this game a lot! She didn't do too well in the last game, so she's been practicing a lot. She's feeling kind of nervous, but she's thinking, I hope the coach gives me a chance to show what I can do now!

Once you've modeled these visualization and discussion strategies, students can work with partners to use them to develop other characters. As a metacognitive activity, you might want to call students together to ask them what they have learned about their characters in this way.

THIRD ASSIGNMENT
Prewriting

To help students get to know their characters even better, duplicate and pass out the worksheet on the next page.

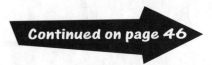

Continued on page 46

Name_____

INTERVIEWING YOUR STORY CHARACTER

The questionnaire below isn't for *you*. It's for your story character! Think about how that character would fill in the blanks. Then write the character's responses.

Character's Name: _____

1. Something I am very good at: _____

_____

2. Something I am *not* very good at: _____

_____

3. My favorite memory from a while ago: _____

_____

4. My *worst* memory from a while ago: _____

_____

5. I get angry when: _____

_____

6. I get sad when: _____

_____

7. Here are some things that make me *very* happy: _____

_____

_____

8. A wonderful thing I would like to happen to me: _____

_____

_____

More To Try! → **What else would you like to ask this story character? Work with a partner to think of some more questions and answers.**

FOURTH ASSIGNMENT
Prewriting

Show, Don't Tell

In their written descriptions students can aim to present their characters through gestures, actions, and thoughts. The completed questionnaire on page 45 will move students in this direction. Here are some additional strategies to try. If you have time, use them in the sequence shown.(You'll also find ideas for mini-lessons on using specific words on pages 26–27.)

Provide a Model

You might write the following model on the chalkboard or read it aloud. Ask students to figure out the setting, what the character is feeling, and how they know.

> Pam could feel the sweat on her forehead. A cool breeze swept against her as she raced hard for the finish line. Out of the corner of her eye, she could see Brad straining right along beside her. She had to win! She just had to!

Invite students to find and share passages from literature that *show* characters rather then simply tell about them.

Go for the Goal Webs

Suggest that students use their questionnaires to make goal webs for their story characters. Enlarge and display the one on this page as a model (or you can copy it onto the board). As students discuss their completed webs, have them reflect on how the webs not only show the character but also get the action of a story started.

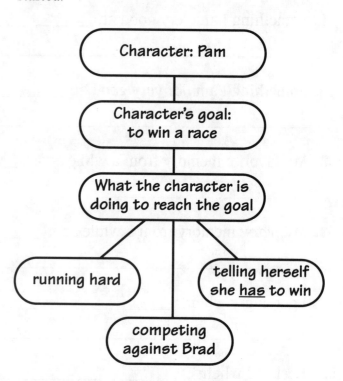

FIFTH ASSIGNMENT
Drafting

Make a First Draft

Invite students to use what they've learned about their story character as they write a paragraph about the character. Remind them that it is effective to picture the character in action. Suggest that students write their drafts in pencil on every other line, so that they can easily revise them.

Be sure to show students the revised draft from Patricia Reilly Giff's *The Candy Corn Contest* on page 25.

SIXTH ASSIGNMENT
Revising and Editing the First Draft

Reviewing work in progress is an important step in the revision process. When students can direct and manage their own writer/editor reviews, they feel more in control of their writng.

Before asking students to conduct writer/editor reviews, have the class develop some guidelines that they feel are important. Summarize and post the class list in your writing center. For example:

1. BE POSITIVE Start by telling something you like about their story character.

2. BE SPECIFIC Point to exact words and sentences you think are especially good. Show just where you think the writing needs improvement.

3. BE HELPFUL Offer clear ideas and suggestions if the writer asks for them. Repeat what the writer says to be sure you understand the problem.

4. BE RESPECTFUL A writer/editor review is a personal conference. These shared thoughts shouldn't go beyond the classroom.

Have a volunteer help you model a writer/editor review. You might also use the form on this page to help the review focus on some definite goals. Make it clear that a writer is free to reject a reviewer's suggestions. Student writer/editors may want to refer to Independent Student Activity on page 65 for revising guidelines.

Reviewing the Review

After the class has had some experience with peer review, you might bring students together to explore these questions:

◆ What are some useful things I've learned from my editor?

◆ How does being an editor help me to improve my own writing?

What Did We Learn?

In closing, explore these questions with the class. Some students may wish to write their answers and include them in their portfolios.

1. What's the easiest way for me to develop a story character?

2. Which of my story characters so far do I like best? Why?

3. What new technique might I try the next time I make up a character for a story?

WRITER'S GOALS

1. What special problem or question do you want your editor to help you figure out? (EXAMPLE: Does my main character seem vivid and real? What else could I show about the character?)

_____

_____

2. Which of your editor's suggestions will help you solve the problem you listed above?

_____

_____

3. As a result of your writer/editor review, what will you do next with your story?

_____

_____

A WHY STORY

For this project students will develop a *pourquoi* story of their own.

Write the word *pourquoi* [poor-KWA] on the chalkboard. Tell students that it is the French word for "why." Ask them to guess what a *pourquoi* story might be. Explain that this is an imaginative way to explain something in nature, such as why an animal has a certain feature or behaves a certain way, why the sky is blue, how something came to be, and so on. Most pourquoi stories are about animals or nature.

Reproduce and distribute this story, *Why There Are Cracks in Turtle's Shell*, to the class to intorduce the genre.

WHY THERE ARE CRACKS IN TURTLE'S SHELL

A *Pourquoi* Story Adapted from an African Folktale

Have you ever wondered why turtles have cracks in their shells? Here's how the Baila tribe in Africa explains it.

Long ago, Turtle and his wife made their home in the reeds of a muddy river. Turtle had many friends who lived up and down the river, but the one he liked best was Buzzard.

However, one day Turtle's wife noticed that Buzzard's visits made her husband sad. "Husband," she said, "what is troubling you?"

Turtle replied, "Don't you see I am becoming hateful in Buzzard's eyes? I know that he is beginning to think that our friendship means nothing to me!"

"Hateful?" said his wife. "Why would your good friend Buzzard ever think that? After all, he comes to see you almost every day!"

"Ah, Wife! That's exactly my point! It is so rude for me not to visit Buzzard. He always comes here, yet I have never been to his house!" Turtle answered.

"Well," said Turtle's wife, "I don't see why that would upset Buzzard. After all, he lives on the top of a high peak. Unless you had wings to fly, how could you ever reach his house?"

"Wings or not, I am sure that Buzzard thinks I should visit him," replied Turtle.

"Well, then," said his wife, "why don't you do something about it? Sprout some wings and fly to visit your friend Buzzard!"

"Don't be silly!" snapped Turtle. "You know I can't do that."

"I'm sure you will find a way," came the response. "You always do."

Turtle pulled his head inside his shell and began to think. Several hours passed, and finally he had an idea. "Wife, I've come up with a plan. I want you to tie me up in a parcel with some rope. When Buzzard arrives, you must pretend that we are starving. Then give him the bundle and say that he should trade it to get some grain for us."

So just before Buzzard was due to arrive, Turtle's wife took some cloth and tied Turtle into a big parcel. Then she dragged it over into the corner.

At his usual time, Buzzard came to call. When Turtle's wife came to the door, he asked, "Where's my friend Turtle?"

"Why, he's out trying to find us some food. We haven't a bit of grain in the house," said Turtle's wife.

"That's trouble, indeed, if you're out of grain," said Buzzard.

"Buzzard, is there any grain to be bought near your house?"

"Why, there is. We have no grain shortage up on the peak."

Upon hearing Buzzard's reply, Turtle's wife pointed to the large parcel in the corner. "My husband left this hoping that you could trade it for some grain. Would you do that?"

Buzzard nodded his head. "Of course, I'd be happy to help out my good friends." Then he looped the parcel over his beak and took off for his home in the heights. As he was nearing the top of the cliff, he was surprised to hear a voice coming from the parcel. It said, "Untie me, Buzzard. I am your friend Turtle. I promised that someday I would pay a visit to your house!"

But Buzzard was so shocked to hear Turtle's voice that he let go of the parcel. Down, down, down it fell until it crashed into the rocks below. The soft rope helped cushion Turtle's fall, but his shell was chipped and broken. (And so was his friendship with Buzzard.) If you look at a turtle's back today, you can still see the cracks in its shell. (And if you ask whether turtles and buzzards are friends, the answer will be no.)

Discuss the story with the class. Ask students what they were thinking as they read the story. Did they think that Buzzard might have something to do with why Turtle has cracks in his shell? When they got to the part about Turtle's plan to get to Buzzard's house, did they guess whay might happen? What did they think about the ending? Can they explain why this is a *pourquoi* story?

Getting Started

Tell students that they are going to develop, draft, revise, and present their own *pourquoi* on a topic of their choice. But first, to reinforce what they've learned about the genre and to help them get started, read aloud the following story, *Why the Sky Is Far Away,* and analyze it in a whole-class discussion. This Bini story from Nigeria is another example of a *pourquoi* story.

> Long ago, Sky lived near Earth. At that time, people didn't farm or draw water or make cooking fires. They just tore off a chunk of Sky and ate it. But people would take too much and throw the extra away. This made Sky angry. He warned the people not to waste his precious gifts.
>
> For a time the people were careful. But at the feast for King Oba, people forgot Sky's warning. One woman tore off a piece of Sky to eat, but it was too big to finish. She tried not to waste it, so she asked her husband to eat some. But he was too full from the day's feasting. So the woman asked her children to help her finish the piece of Sky. But they were too full. So were all the neighbors. So the woman threw the extra piece of Sky in the garbage.
>
> At that moment, Sky grew dark. Thunder and lightning shook as Sky's angry voice roared out. "You have wasted the gifts of nature. I, Sky, will move away. You will

> have to find your own food. Then you'll learn not to be wasteful." Sky floated up, far beyond the people's reach.
>
> This is why the sky is far away and people must find their own food.

Talking About the Task

Invite students to respond to the *pourquoi* story *Why the Sky Is Far Away*. Have them identify the characteristic of nature it attempts to explain. Point out that not only does this pourquoi story tell why the sky is so far from Earth, it also teaches a lesson. Can students tell in their own words what that lesson is? *(People must be careful with the gifts that nature provides.)*

When discussing the tale with the class, you might ask:

◆ What is the purpose of the opening paragraph?

◆ How would you describe Sky?

◆ How did the woman react when she knew her piece of Sky was too big?

◆ Suppose you wanted to revise this *pourquoi* story. How might you change it? What would you add?

The activities that follow will help students through the process of writing their own *pourquoi* story.

FIRST ASSIGNMENT
Prewriting Discussion

One way to help students create *pourquoi* stories is to immerse them in the genre. Consult with your school or community librarian for help in gathering a selection. Under the Dewey Decimal system these stories are catalogued as folklore with the call number 398.2. Here are some books you might look for:

◆ *Why the Crab Has No Head* retold by Barbara Knutson

◆ *Why the Tides Ebb and Flow* by Joan Chase Bowden

◆ *Why the North Star Stands Still and Other Indian Legends* by William R. Palmer

◆ *Why the Possum's Tail Is Bare and Other North American Indian Nature Tales* collected by James E. Connolly

Reading Before Writing

As a prewriting activity, have each student read one or two *pourquoi* stories, preferably from different cultures. Divide the class into small discussion groups. Within the groups, students can read their stories independently or take turns reading them aloud to the group. Ask students to take turns sharing the stories in their own words and listing some ideas about them to contribute to a full-class discussion.

Bring the whole class together. List the different cultures represented by the stories students read. You may want to indicate the range of cultures on a chart or map. Then discuss some of the common characteristics that students noticed among the *pourquoi* stories:

◆ What characteristics of animals or nature do the stories explain?

◆ Why do you think people tell stories like these?

◆ What moods do the stories convey: are they serious, humorous, scary, encouraging?

◆ Do any of the *pourquoi* stories have a message? What are the messages?

SECOND ASSIGNMENT
Choosing a Topic

Have students choose a topic for their *pourquoi* story. This task will come easily to some students. Others, however, may need help to find a topic that sparks their imagination. Brainstorm possible topics or try this hands-on technique.

Idea Spinners

Have students make two spinners like the ones shown here. Each spinner can be cut from oak tag or cardboard. Use a brass paper fastener to attach a paper clip to the center as the pointer. Make sure the paper clip is loose enough to spin. As an alternative, make a hole in the center of the spinner and poke a pencil through it. Roll the spinner on the desktop until it stops. The part of the spinner that touches the desk is the one to use.

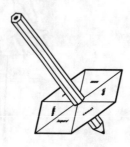

Explain that each spinner presents words or phrases that could go together to suggest a topic for a *pourquoi* story. Students spin both spinners to generate a random combination, such as *Why we fear* and *shark*. This can suggest a topic for a possible *pourquoi* story: *Why Humans Are Afraid of Sharks.* Or the idea could be adjusted for a story called *Why Sharks Have Such Scary Teeth.*

If a student does not like the combination that comes up, he or she spins one or both of the idea spinners again until a more desirable combination comes up. Encourage students to customize the idea spinners by changing the words or phrases they contain, or by providing more or fewer sections.

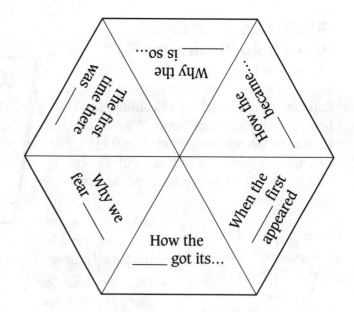

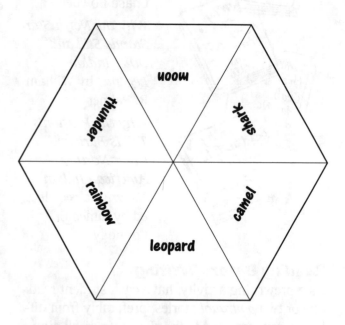

THIRD ASSIGNMENT
Prewriting

In the third assignment, students complete the chart on the next page for their *pourquoi* stories. Before passing out the worksheet, you might reread the tale *Why the Sky Is Far Away* on page 50.

Continued on page 54

Name_____

CHART THE CHANGES

Most *pourquoi* stories begin with an animal or a feature of nature presented in a certain way. Then something happens to cause a change. The result is the way the animal or natural feature is today.

The chart below shows the changes that happen in *Why the Sky Is Far Away.* Study the top chart, then use the empty bottom chart to organize the parts of your own *pourquoi* story.

Before	What Caused the Change	After
Sky lives near Earth. People eat Sky.	People waste Sky. Sky gets angry and warns people. People forget Sky's warning.	Sky moves away. People have to find own food.

Before	What Caused the Change	After

More To Try! → Draw pictures to illustrate the three parts of your chart.

FOURTH ASSIGNMENT
Drafting

A *pourquoi* story needs well-developed characters and a coherent plot. By this point, students should have developed an outline for their story using their charts. Before students begin drafting, use the following checklists to help them sharpen the details of character and plot. (If they are still having trouble developing a logical plot, consider having them work on the Independent Student Activity on plot structure on page 62.)

Who?

Write the following questions on the chalkboard for students to consider as they develop the *characters* in their *pourquoi* story:

◆ Who is the main character?

◆ How would you describe this character: good, evil, sly, weak, curious, boastful, powerful?

◆ What does the character say or do to show this quality?

◆ Who or what else participates in the story: a trickster, god, magician, spirit, queen, animal, element of nature (volcano, snow, sunlight, thunder)?

What?

Write these questions on the chalkboard for students to consider as they work through the *plot* of their *pourquoi* story. Remind students that a good plot has a clear *turning point* that results in the final outcome.

◆ What change will take place?

◆ Why will the change happen?

◆ How will it happen? Is there an injury? Is there an argument or fight? Does a newcomer arrive? Does someone leave?

TEACHER TIP
Students who need help with plot might describe the main character as it really exists, and then work backward. For instance, if they want to write about why the kangaroo has a pouch, they can first find out the purpose of a kangaroo's pouch, and then think of fanciful explanations to use in their story.

What Else?

What is the outcome of the *pourquoi* story? These questions can help students figure out how to bring their story to an end:

◆ Who benefits from what happens?

◆ Who loses?

◆ What punishment is given?

◆ What lesson is learned?

You can present these questions on chart paper, work with students in small conference groups, or have them work with partners to pull together their ideas.

Putting Pen to Paper

Now it's time for students to set their ideas down in a first draft. Have students begin their drafts in class and, if necessary, complete them over several days. Allow time for writing conferences in which you guide students, as needed, through problems they encounter as they draft.

FIFTH ASSIGNMENT
Revising and Editing

Some students will start revising their work as soon as they write their first sentence. Others will need guidance to carry out this process. You'll find some classroom-tested guidelines for revising with a peer on page 47 in Project 1. You'll also want to direct students to the Independent Student Activity on revising (page 65) and on editing (page 66). Here are a few tips to make these processes easier for students:

◆ Suggest that students read their work aloud to hear how it sounds. Does the dialogue "ring true"? Can they hear tense or transition problems?

◆ Provide self-stick notes or highlighter pens for students to mark sections that need attention.

◆ Suggest that students use a ruler so they can edit one line at a time.

Presenting

Have students prepare a final draft of their *pourquoi* stories by hand or on the computer. Invite them to add illustrations if they wish. Students might present their stories to small groups. Each group might then choose one person's story to present to the whole class. You might also display students' stories on a bulletin board. (See the suggestions on page 16.)

Another way to present *pourquoi* stories is to bind them together into a notebook. Talk with the school librarian about adding this collection to the folklore section of your library. You might also have a folklore day, in which students share their *pourquoi* stories, act out *pourquoi* stories from different cultures, and serve food from around the world. (Additional ideas for sharing work appear on pages 67 and 68.)

Extension: Tale Twisting

Some students may enjoy writing another *pourquoi* story, but with an unexpected twist. Suggest that they create "*Pourquoi*? **NOT!**" stories as a variation on this genre. They would take an animal or element of nature as it really is and explain an imaginary change that is impossible, such as "How the Pig Got Its Trunk" or "Why Ice Flows from Volcanoes."

What Did We Learn?

In closing, explore some of these questions with the class. You might conduct an oral discussion or ask students to write their answers in their notebooks or journals.

◆ What process did I go through in writing this story?

◆ What did I learn from writing this story?

◆ What do I like best about this work?

◆ What might I do differently next time?

POURQUOI STORY EXTENSIONS— THINKING AND DRAWING

After the class has read and written *pourquoi* stories, you might use the experience as a springboard for other creative writing activities.

Pass-Along Stories

Whole-group oral storytelling is an easy way to get students in a storytelling mood. This technique is especially effective after you've shared a story derived from oral tradition, such as "Why There Are Cracks in Turtle's Shell" or other folk- or fairy tales. Before forming a storytelling circle, engage students in a brainstorming session to come up with some storytelling topics similar to the story you've just shared. As they're offered, record these story-starter ideas on slips of paper and place them in a bag. After everyone has gathered in a storytelling circle, ask a student to select a slip from the bag and read it aloud. Then you or a volunteer can launch the story. The next person in the circle picks up on the story where the first storyteller left off. Continue passing along the story until someone brings it to a conclusion or runs out of ideas. If the latter occurs, others in the group may want to give a prompt or suggestion; if the story has reached a dead-end, which sometimes happens, the storyteller can select another story-starter idea from the bag.

Another Story

Remind students of how Turtle's cracks are explained in "Why There Are Cracks in Turtle's Shell" (pages 48–49). Then ask them to think of other explanations. List students' ideas on the board and challenge them to write their own versions of this tale.

Symbol Stories

Draw the symbol shown here on the chalkboard and tell the class that it stands for Turtle. Then copy the symbol sentence and ask students to "read" it. After several students have shared their versions, explain that there is no one right answer. Students can use the symbols to stand for whatever they like. Challenge students to use the symbols to tell a tale about Turtle.

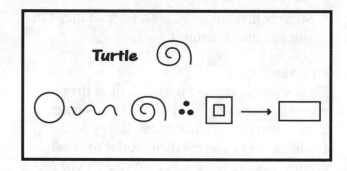

Stories Behind the Headlines

Ask students to bring from home some recent local newspapers. As they browse through the papers, ask them to be on the lookout for interesting headlines. After clipping a headline, encourage students to write a paragraph explaining *why* this event occurred. Suggest that students save the real articles so they can compare their fanciful *pourquoi* stories to the news.

INDEPENDENT STUDENT ACTIVITIES...

...that students can do when they have time or as needed

STORY PROMPTS

Getting started is sometimes the hardest part of writing. Here's a list of story starter ideas. Choose one of them to begin your story.

1. A cranky queen forbids laughing in her kingdom. Write a story about what happens when a clown comes to town.

2. You are working in the library, and one of the books begins to talk. What does it say? What do you do? Does anyone else find out what's going on?

3. On the way to the dentist, you meet a unicorn. What do you both say and do? Write a story about this meeting.

4. Write a mysterious story with this title: "The Case of Mr. McCloskey's Disappearing Dentures."

5. You've been invited to the White House to meet the President! The two of you sit down to chat in the Rose Garden, when a very funny thing happens. Write about it.

6. During a hike in the woods, you spot an odd-looking shed made from planks of woods, logs, mud, and old tires. You open the crooked, creaking door and are startled to see...

7. An absolutely unbelievable thing has just happened! Write a letter to a real or imagined friend to tell *all* about it.

8. You have been reading *Alice in Wonderland*. All of a sudden, you, too, are just a few inches tall. Describe your adventures as a miniperson.

9. When you clean out your dresser drawer, you find a most unusual watch. Tell what kind of time it keeps and how this affects what you do for a day.

10. Oh, no! One day, when you come to school, you are invisible to your teacher and classmates. Describe what happens during this time.

IDEAS FROM AUTHORS

Where can you get ideas for writing? How can you improve your writing? Here are some suggestions from well-known authors.

1. Friendly Help

Think of somebody who you really like, and then think of the worst problem he or she could possibly have. How could you help solve that problem?

from Walter Dean Myers, author of *Fallen Angels*

2. Experience the Emotion

I always tell would-be writers to search their own memories for a time when they experienced a strong emotion: fear, anger, joy, sorrow, guilt. How, as a result of the experience that created that emotion, did they change? There is where a story lies.

from Lois Lowry, author of *Number the Stars*

3. Record Your Thoughts

Keep a journal. Use it to help you learn to write. Proper use of language shapes one's thinking.... The discipline of writing hones thinking skills.

from E.L. Konigsburg, author of *From the Mixed-Up Files of Mrs. Basil E. Frankweiler*

4. Lead with a Letter

Write a letter. If you want to tell a story and you don't know how to begin and you're flopping around and don't know what to do and it's all vague, put it in the form of a letter. Write a letter to Shakespeare if you want. "Dear Bill, I'm working on a story, and I'm trying to..." All of a sudden, before you know what you're doing, you're into the story.

from Lloyd Alexander, author of *The High King*

5. Views of News

Chop a couple dozen news stories out of a week's daily papers. Shuffle them around and try to compose a story out of any three or four.

from Joan Aiken, author of *The Wolves of Willoughby Chase*

6. Begin with a Book

Take the first sentence of the next book you were going to read. Write your own story based on that sentence. Then read the book.

from Cynthia Voight, author of *Dicey's Song*

STORY TOSS GAME

Here's a storytelling game to play with two of your friends.

Materials:
3 sheets of duplicating paper ◆ markers
◆ scissors ◆ tape

Steps:

1. Begin by tracing and cutting out three copies of the cube pattern on this page.

2. Work together to brainstorm the following:
   - ◆ 6 different characters
   - ◆ 6 different story settings
   - ◆ 6 different story problems

3. Record your characters on the six sides of one cube. Make cubes with the story setting and problem lists too.

4. Then fold along the dotted lines and tape the edges to finish your cubes.

5. Take turns rolling the three cubes. Now the fun begins! Weave a story around the character, setting, and story problem that appear.

More to Try!

Try rolling the cubes two or three times instead of once. What kind of story can you create with multiple characters, settings, and story problems?

BRAINSTORMING

Brainstorming—what a funny word! What do you think it means? If you have a storm in your brain, then thoughts must fly in all directions. Sometimes these ideas can be harnessed for a story. When you brainstorm for a writing project, you let the ideas flow. Here are three brainstorming techniques to try.

Freewriting

In freewriting, start with a topic and just write whatever comes to mind about it.

◆ First write down your topic. It can be just a single word.

◆ Without stopping, write anything you think of about the topic.

◆ If you can't think of anything to write, just write your topic, over and over, until an idea does jump into your head.

◆ Time yourself. For example, you can freewrite for three minutes.

◆ You can freewrite more than once. For example, write for a few minutes, then stop and turn to another task. When you return, add to what you wrote the first time.

◆ Later, reread what you wrote. Is there a story idea?

> **TIP**
> You may also find it helpful to use more than one brainstorming strategy for the same writing topic.

Idea Web

Idea webs are diagrams that show connections among ideas.

◆ Choose a subject. Write your subject in the center of a page and circle it.

◆ Write any words or main ideas related to your subject. Circle them and connect them to the subject with a line. Keep going until you run out of main ideas.

◆ Add details about each main idea. Link them to the idea with lines.

Here is part of an idea web on the topic of *inventions:*

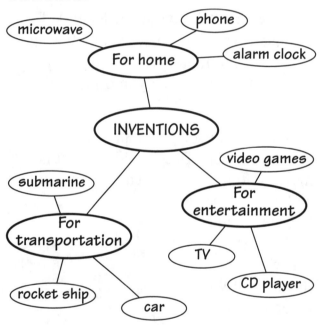

Word Mountains

Here's another way to get started. With this strategy, focus on developing one idea.

◆ Start with an interesting word.

◆ Add an adjective or describing word.

◆ Add more words for each line. How many details can you add to your word mountain?

mess
colorful mess
colorful mess in my room
Dad's opinion about colorful mess in my room

WHAT'S HAPPENING

To avoid plot snarls like the one in the cartoon, many writers work out their story plots ahead of time. Here are two plotting strategies.

1. Make an "Excitement Profile"

Brainstorm and list some exciting events that you want to happen in your story. Put the events in any order you think of them. Letter the events.

Arrange your events on a profile like the one shown here. Decide which event is the most exciting. That should come near the end. On this profile the writer decided that **b** was the most exciting. Do you see where **b** is on the profile? Why do you think the writer put **d** after **b**? Decide which events are the least exciting. They should come toward the beginning. This writer thought that **c**, **a**, and **e** were the least exciting events, so they are first on the graph.

a. The ET lands on a farm and scares the cows.

b. Government agents chase the ET into a subway.

c. Maybe the ET arrives in a craft that looks like a school bus.

d. The ET could be rescued by some kids.

e. The ET joins some human kids on a field trip to the city.

2. Make a Plot Staircase

The first event is step #1. The last step is the story ending. Fill in those two steps first. Then fill in the other steps to show how they lead from first to last. Here's an example:

4. They both get a prize!

3. The bug goes <u>higher</u>, to the top of the tree.

2. The horse goes <u>faster</u>.

1. A bug challenges a horse to a race. The finish line is a tree.

Work with a partner. Make a plot staircase and an excitement profile for a story you want to write together. How do these strategies give you even more ideas for your story?

c a e b d

STORY MIDDLES

You might think of a story as a sandwich. It has three main parts: the beginning, middle, and end. Sandwiched between the beginning and the end is the meat of the story—the middle. The activities on this page will help you write meatier middles.

Draw It Out

Try this activity with a partner. Fold two pieces of paper so you have six or eight squares in each piece. Number the squares. Draw two animals or people in the first square. Draw the same characters in the last square, but show them doing something different. Then exchange papers with your partner. Fill in the missing squares with pictures or words to create a story middle.

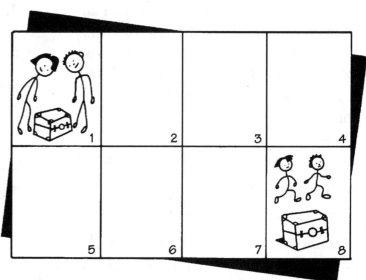

The big house on the hill was empty. That was fine with the squirrels, chipmunks, and birds. An empty house meant no people, no lawn mowers, no gardeners, no danger. Even the deer from the nearby woods enjoyed grazing on the wide lawn. The house was empty for so long that the animals almost forgot what a nuisance people could be.

Write a Dagwood

A cartoon character named Dagwood is known for putting lots of filling into his sandwiches. On a sheet of paper, draw an outline of a Dagwood sandwich like the one shown here. Then fill it with the middle of this story.

So from then on, the animals stayed in the field and forest. But once in a while, when the moon was new, they'd slip closer to the house because, after all, it had once been theirs.

AUDIENCE AND PURPOSE

Writing is a lot like talking. You need words for both. But there are some differences. For example, when you're talking, you usually can see whom you're talking to.

You probably talk differently to a small baby than you do to a strict uncle or to your best friend. When you are writing, you can't see the person who will be reading your work. You have to imagine who the reader or readers will be. Good writers spend some time imagining their readers or audience before they begin to write.

Audiences can be:

- a special friend
- another class
- yourself
- adults at home
- your classmates and teacher
- readers of a children's magazine
- neighbors
- a younger child
- contest judges

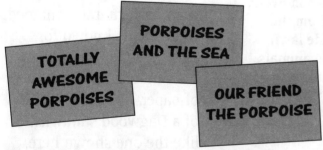

TOTALLY AWESOME PORPOISES

PORPOISES AND THE SEA

OUR FRIEND THE PORPOISE

The "Write" Audience

Pretend you are an expert on porpoises and a very busy one. Right now you're working on three books at once: one for teenagers, one for kindergartners, and one for scientists. It's time to mail the pages to your publishers, but they're all mixed up. Take a look at these pages and decide which one is for each of your books.

Try This Choose three different audiences from the list on this page. Write a book title about the same topic for each audience.

Writing for a Purpose

Whether they're writing about dolphins or dinosaurs, writers always have a purpose.

Some purposes are:

- to explain something (In a pourquoi story you explain how something came to be.)
- to describe something (You might describe a character, setting, mood, or adventure.)
- to entertain or amuse (Your story might give pleasure or be really funny.)
- to persuade someone (You might suggest or describe ideas or plans that others will do, too.)

Try This Work with a partner. Find at least four different kinds of writing. You might look at books, magazines,  newspapers, and other materials in your classroom, the library, or at home. Decide what the purpose of each is.

MAKING IT BETTER

When you revise, you read your work again with "new eyes." Sometimes it is helpful to have a partner's "new eyes" too. Take turns reading your story. Then go over it together. Here's a checklist to use as you reread the story. Use a colored pencil to mark the parts of the draft that you want to revise.

Reading-Partner Checklist

1. Does the story have a good beginning? Does it make me want to read more? Make a ✔ if the beginning needs work.

2. Is the plot of the story easy to follow? If there are parts of the plot that are out of order or aren't clear, circle them lightly.

3. Who is the main character? What do I like best about this character?

4. What words or phrases in the story are especially colorful and descriptive? Put a ! in the margin next to them.

5. Are there words that are overused or too general? Draw a line lightly under them. Suggest some replacement words in the margin.

6. Are there places where the story is too wordy, or where the same thing is said over and over again? Circle them lightly.

7. What is your favorite part of this story? Be ready to tell the author why you like this part.

After you and your partner have both finished reading, get together and discuss your checklist ideas. Then revise your own story. Follow these revision tips.

Writer's Revision Tips

1. Decide which of your reading partner's suggestions you want to use. You may like all of them, or just a few.

2. What new ideas do *you* have for improving your story? Make some notes about them on your draft.

3. When you've finished revising your story, go on to editing it. Some editing tips are on page 66.

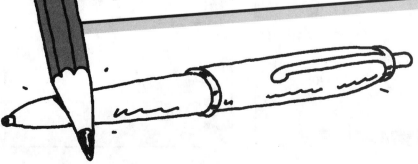

DOTTING THE I'S AND CROSSING THE T'S

You've written your first draft and made revisions. Now it's time to proofread and edit your work.

Here are some tips to make the editing job easier and faster.

1. Skip lines when you write your draft. That way you'll have room to write in changes and corrections.

2. Use a different color pencil or pen to mark your corrections. It will be easier to spot changes.

3. Be sure to date your edited work. That way you know which is the latest version. (This is especially important if you use a computer to print out your drafts!)

4. Use an editing checklist like the one shown here. Edit for just one thing at a time.

5. Use the proofreading symbols shown here. Copy them onto an index card and use it to help you keep your place as you edit.

Editing Checklist

1. Check for capital and lowercase letters. Does each sentence begin with a capital letter? Did you capitalize proper nouns?

2. Check for punctuation. Does each sentence end correctly? Did you use commas and quotation marks correctly?

3. Check for spelling errors. Circle any words that may be misspelled. Look them up in the dictionary or use your computer's spell-checker.

4. Check your paragraphs. Does each paragraph contain a main idea?

5. Check to see if you've overused a word. Can you think of a different way to say the same thing?

Proofreading Marks

∧	insert
⊙	period
⌄?	question mark
∧,	comma
⌄'	apostrophe
⌄"	quotation marks
¶	paragraph indent
≡	capital letter
/	lowercase letter
sp◯	spell correctly
℘	delete (take out)
↻	move
∿	transpose (switch order)
#	insert space
⊂	take out space

MAKING A BOOK

The shapes and forms of your books can be as creative as your stories. Here are book-making ideas you might try.

Story Corral

Round up your best story idea and use it to make this hanging display.

Materials:

writing paper ◆ crayons or markers ◆ 3 sheets of 9-inch by 12-inch construction paper ◆ glue ◆ stapler ◆ yarn ◆ scissors

Steps:

1. Copy your story onto three pieces of writing paper. Add some illustrations if you have space.

2. Glue your three story pages onto the construction paper. Try to place each page so that you have even borders around the writing paper.

3. Stand up the story pages to form a story corral. (Be sure that you've put the pages in the correct order so your story can be read in sequence by turning the corral clockwise.) Get a partner to help you staple the edges of the paper together.

4. Place your story corral on a tabletop as part of a display or make a hanging corral. To do this, punch a hole in the center near the top of each page and attach a piece of yarn. Bring the three pieces of yarn together and tie a knot to make a hanger. Then display your story corral at eye level.

Fan-Paged Book

This type of book works well for stories that have separate parts.

Materials:

7 sheets of 8½-inch by 11-inch duplicating paper ◆ pencil ◆ ruler ◆ scissors ◆ stapler ◆ construction paper ◆ crayons

Steps:

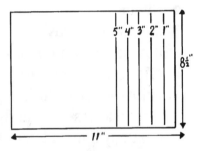

1. Use the ruler to measure and mark a 1-inch segment on one piece of duplicating paper. Cut off this strip so you have a piece of paper 8½ inches by 10 inches in size.

2. Repeat, cutting off a 2-inch strip, a 3-inch strip, and so on so your pages will make a fan book.

3. Stack the set of pages together, then add a construction paper cover and staple the pages and the cover along the left-hand side.

4. Write your story inside your fan book. Add illustrations if you like.

PUBLISHING

Publishing is the way you choose to share your finished work with others. Here are a few ideas for publishing your work, but remember, this list is just a starting point. Have fun thinking of even more ideas of your own.

◆ Tape-record your story. Consider adding some sound effects or mood music to go with what you have written.

◆ Practice retelling your story, then share it with a small group in your class or arrange to be a visiting storyteller and tell your story to younger students.

◆ Divide your story into short installments. Each day, post another section of it on a bulletin board for others to read. (Try to choose exciting stopping points—called cliffhangers—so that your readers can hardly wait until the next day's installment.)

◆ Do a video presentation of your story. You might want to wear a costume or ask some classmates to help you perform your story as a play or a reader's theater.

◆ Dress like one of the characters in your story. Then give a sneak preview telling what the story is about without giving away the ending. Be ready to share your story with interested classmates.

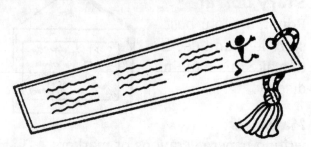

◆ If you've written a poem, consider making a poetry bookmark. Copy your poem on a 3-inch by 8-inch piece of tagboard. Use crayons or markers to decorate the border or add an illustration. Add a yarn tassel at the top. For extra durability, laminate your bookmark or cover it with clear contact paper.

◆ Make a poster advertising your story. As part of your advertisement, tell your classmates how they can get a copy of your story to read.

◆ Try doing a flannel board or puppet show retelling of your story. Or, as you read your story, use simple props or hand motions to go with your story text.

◆ Contribute your story to a class newspaper or literary magazine. You might wish to draw a picture to appear with your selection.

◆ Create your own book by stapling your story pages inside construction paper covers.

You'll find more book ideas on page 67.

TEACHER'S NOTEBOOK...

...including tips on assessment, technology, and a
bibliography of books written for students and teachers

PORTFOLIO AND ASSESSMENT IDEAS

The act of creative writing provides an ideal forum for students to focus on process as well as product. By retracing and thinking about the steps they used to create one piece of work, students can find strategies to use in all their writing.

Portfolios of Progress: How My Story Came to Be

Have students make a sequential file. Ask them to keep all those notes, pictures, word lists, and strategies that are part of their prewriting work. Next in the sequence can come the writer's first drafts and notes made during a partner revision session. Finally comes the finished story.

Invite students to share with a small group their process materials. As a framework for the group discussion, ask students to focus on these questions as they show their portfolio materials:

◆ Why did I do this step?

◆ What did I learn from it?

◆ How did this step help me to write a good story?

◆ How can I use a step like this the next time I write?

Assessing Progress

To show students the importance you attach to process, you can use two types of conferencing.

The Roving Conference This is where you move around the classroom as children are involved in their writing tasks. You might ask a student: "What are you writing?" "What do you want to do next?" Note students' responses and make notes about any significant behaviors, problems, and successes. The roving conference also offers you a chance to "slip in" with a student and offer support and encouragement as needed.

The Individual Conference In this teacher-student conversation, you and the writer talk about the work in progress. You can make observational notes that will help later in evaluation. Here is a possible sequence of conference steps:

1. The student reads what she or he has written. The teacher listens and observes style, content, and organization.

2. The teacher summarizes the piece of writing. The student tells whether the teacher has "gotten the message."

3. The teacher tells what is interesting in the writing, then asks questions about details and organization.

4. The teacher asks the student to think about what details he or she would like to add, or about material that might be deleted.

5. The teacher focuses on what the student has done correctly. This might be, for example, spelling, punctuation, or word choice.

6. Teacher and student discuss what the student will do next with the piece of writing. The teacher helps the student set one or two important goals. Clarity may be the biggest goal.

As you can see, the aims of the individual conference are to work with the writer to (1) identify the strong points of the story in progress and (2) set specific goals for the next part of the process.

TECHNO-HINTS

Your students can take advantage of technology in many ways to stimulate and refine their creative writing skills. Here are some suggestions for using valuable tools in your writing program.

> **TEACHER TIP**
> Enlist the aid of a parent volunteer to offer computer help at predetermined times each week.

Word Processing

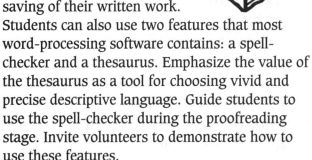

Students who have had opportunities to use word processors can readily appreciate the benefits of easy drafting, revising, editing, and saving of their written work.

Students can also use two features that most word-processing software contains: a spell-checker and a thesaurus. Emphasize the value of the thesaurus as a tool for choosing vivid and precise descriptive language. Guide students to use the spell-checker during the proofreading stage. Invite volunteers to demonstrate how to use these features.

> **TEACHER TIP**
> Post a list of student names and a timer next to your computer(s) each day or week. Explain that only students on the list can use the computer, and they must set the timer for the length of time you designate.

CD-ROM

Students who have access to computers with CD-ROM drives and a library of CD-ROM software have many opportunities to get inspiration for writing from the visual images they can find as they browse.

> **TEACHER TIP**
> Work out a procedure with students for protecting and caring for the equipment in your classroom.

On-Line Capability

If your school is on-line, your students may be able to interact with "cyberpeers" in schools all across the country. They can exchange information and personal perspectives, offer writing ideas, share stories, poetry, and essays, and get feedback on what they've written. Your students can even work together on joint projects with students in other locations.

Audio- and Videotape Recorders

Students can use audiocassette recorders as a way to keep track of brainstorming sessions. They also can use them to listen to what they've written. For example, have students tape an oral reading of a story in progress. As they play it back, they can listen to the language, style, or flow to decide whether these ring true for the intended audience.

> **TEACHER TIP**
> Have students take turns being "techno-tutors." Each tutor shares with a classmate word processing knowledge or skill with a camcorder. Post a list so that everyone gets a chance to learn and to teach.

If available, students might use video camcorders to present their finished work. For instance, students can make a video clip of a local setting that fits their piece, such as a walk through the woods, a supermarket, or a sports event. Students can play the video while they read their story aloud.

Students who make audio- or videotapes to accompany their written work may choose to include them in their portfolios.

BIBLIOGRAPHY

TEACHER RESOURCES

The Art of Teaching Writing by Lucy M. Calkins (Heinemann)

Better Than Book Reports by Christine Boardman Moen (Scholastic)

Creative Writing Schoolhouse Sillies by Joy Patten and Elaine Pelosi (Frank Schaffer)

Everyone Write series, *425 Creative Writing Ideas,* and *Best Writing Activities* by Linda Ward Beech (Sniffen Court Books)

A Fresh Look at Writing and *Writing: Teachers & Children at Work* by Donald H. Graves (Heinemann)

Inviting Children's Authors and Illustrators by Kathy East (Neal-Schulman)

Journaling by Karen Bromley (Scholastic)

Meet the Authors and Illustrators, Vols. I and II by Deborah Kovacs and James Preller (Scholastic)

Meet the Authors of Upper Elementary and Middle School Books by Deborah Kovacs (Scholastic)

150 Thematic Writing Activities by Tara McCarthy (Scholastic)

Read! Write! Publish! by Barbara Fairfax and Adela Garcia (Creative Teaching Press)

75 Creative Ways to Publish Students' Writing by Cherilyn Sunflower (Scholastic)

Teaching Writing A Workshop Approach by Adele Fiderer (Scholastic)

Think! Draw! Write! by Jean Marzollo and Katherine M. Widner (Fearon)

325 Creative Prompts for Personal Journals by J. A. Senn (Scholastic)

Writing Power Plus by Deborah Akers and Von McInnis (Fearon)

The Write Stuff by John Artman (Good Apple)

Writing Crafts Workshop by Bonnie Bernstein (Fearon)

STUDENT RESOURCES

Author's Own Stories About Writing

Best Wishes by Cynthia Rylant (Owen)

A Bookworm Who Hatched by Verna Aardema (Owen)

Dear Mr. Henshaw by Beverly Cleary (William Morrow)

Ezra Jack Keats: Artist and Picture Book Maker by Brian Alderson (Pelican)

Homesick: My Own Story by Jean Fritz (Putnam)

Invincible Louisa by Cornelia Meigs (Scholastic)

A Letter from Phoenix Farm by Jane Yolen (Owen)

Lives of the Writers and What the Neighbors Thought by Kathleen Krull (Harcourt)

The Moon and I by Betsy Byars (Messner)

A Storyteller's Story by Rafe Martin (Owen)

The Writing Bug by Lee Bennett Hopkins (Owen)

How-To Books About Writing

How a Book Is Made by Aliki (Bantam)

Writing a Fact and Fun Book by Amanda Lewis (Kids Can Press)

SOFTWARE

Creative Writer™ (Microsoft)

My Own Stories™ (MECC)